THE FIFTH FIFTY POEMS

●●●●●

Jenefer Ann Murray

Published by Palores Publications 2010

The Fifth Fifty Poems

Front Cover:

ISBN 978-1-906845-16-2

Published by:
Palores Publications,
11a Penryn Street,
Redruth,
Cornwall.
TR15 2SP

Designed and printed by:
ImageSet,
63 Tehidy Road,
Camborne,
Cornwall.
TR10 8LJ

Typeset in:
Helvetica 11pt
Helvetica 14pt

However modest our stories are we can derive greater insights from ourselves than from all the books of old, only an intimidating scholarly culture makes us think otherwise.

Alain de Botton from an essay on Michel de Montaigne.

CONTENTS

Empty Head

Woke up in morning
lay abed
took a look inside my head
in case
there might be poem awaiting
but no
there wasn't, not then
almost
went to sleep again
but I
was, of course, unfed
later
later, ah, poems arrive
and quite
a number, four or five

good morning, good day.

Small Car

Daddy's first car after he was wed
before that motor bike or father's Wolseley
now, ABC, open two seater
bright green, new toy, like wife
whom he dearly loved, all his life.

interesting arrangement, curious
on dashboard, oil drip and pump
oil dripped slowly, slowly, fascinating
if it stopped, bad news, trouble
quick, employ pump on the double.

Daddy spent a lot of time under car
with his legs sticking out
sometimes called in on him from garden
see how he was getting on
but he never answered, not once

when he wanted to discover
how it was now, the car,
he took it for a drive to find out
sometimes took me too
to keep an eye on the oil

but I was not of responsible age
attention easily diverted
"oo look Daddy pretty flowers."
"oil darling oil."
"oo look daddy, geese."

"keep your eye on the oil, missis."
"oo look daddy, Mrs Treviglos."
"d- bother Mrs Treviglos, how's the oil?"
But we never came to grief
oh no, not once.

Ivy's Headache

One evening when she was very little
Ivy had a headache, quite unusual, quite severe.
Mother had to go out, with Father
to dinner party across the road, quite near
boring people, slightly hearty, waste of time.
Ivy didn't think her mother wanted to go
and Ivy didn't want her to go
but she had to go so she went.

Ivy was left with Nanny, her baby brother
dear old very old Granny, the two maids
faithful aides, nursery fire flickering gently
behind its tall and twinkling brass-edged guard
her teddy bear, dolls, dog, cat, canary in its cage
white mice, didn't like them much
the cat did, though, hungered after them actually
but Ivy wanted her mother and no other
without her the world gaped hugely
beyond door enormous cave full
of black unknown creatures poised to attack.

"I want my Mummy" she wailed despairingly
unable to sleep, too young to count sheep
headache worse with wanting and wailing.
"Oh now, Miss Ivy," they said, coming in relays
cold flannels for forehead*, extremely horrid and torrid
hot milk for throat, sore from screaming.
Granny came slowly, an unguent to anoint
whatever might need it, soothing words beside the point
all of them, all of them, went again dismayed.
"I want Mummy, I want Mummy," Ivy sobbed
without her she felt unfinished, desolate and diminished
thrashing about in bed, sore throat aching head.

Eventually in she came rushing - oh!
flowery chiffon frock, wavy auburn hair
lovely scent, at last at last she was there
"Oh Mummy I wanted you, I did want you so badly."
"Well here I am darling." She had looked after the wounded
in World War 1, been a theatre sister
was somewhat dismissive of minor ailments
but she clasped Ivy in her arms, sat on the bed
looked beautiful, banished the maids, marshalled the toys
directed Nanny's ministrations, the world returned
filled up again and Ivy fell asleep at last.
Next morning, headache gone
although a real headache, not a fake
after that Ivy knew her mother would come if she could
if she didn't it would be because she couldn't
Ivy never had another headache.
An early lesson in the intricacies of infantile sorrows.

**pronounced 'forrid' in this instance.*

Large Car

"We think you ought,"
said our parents
when we trotted in
to say good morning,
"to go and look in the garage."

"In the *garage?* Before *breakfast?"*
But if they wanted us to,
oh well - off we went
and when we got there
we saw at once the reason.

A simply enormous car
made the ABC
look like a small green pea
towered over us
and *that* was not *all.*

It was scarlet and yellow
chassis bright red
mudguards bright yellow
absolutely huge
we were *astonished.*

An Italian car, a Fiat
christened *King Kong* by parents
didn't stay with us long
turned out
it did six or eight to the gallon.

Voisin

After the Fiat another unusual vehicle
French racing car although its name
Voisin, French for neighbour
didn't sound quite right for a racer
even in France but you never know
actually I believe it was the name of the maker
saw it again years later in a motor museum
sudden acute memory flash
think it was the same
couldn't remember registration number
but I'm sure it was the same, think so
only ever seen one, of others not a trace
not on the road, not anywhere.

It weighed two tons, more or less
a hefty creation
had a boat-shaped wooden stern
which housed my brother and me
a radiator mascot, handsome silver wings
adorned its long fern-green bonnet
with a finial flourish, lovely to see
my father wedged a potato between,
informed anyone interested
that potato has done more mileage
than any other potato in the country

It thundered about with us for some years
never remember it breaking down
but one day, one foggy day
my mother driving us to Plymouth
(dancing class a much loved outing
she shopped I danced
then we had tea, two buns for me.)
across Yelverton Moor
not fast because of fog
in a queue, in fact - suddenly a puncture
we whizzed round, a catherine wheel

twice, not hitting anything, what luck,
stopped facing the same way as before
my mother flung her arms around me,
as we spun and cried, “Oh Jenny Jenny.”

I aged six, knowing little of danger
quite unperturbed, all agog in the fog
but my poor mother suspecting she’d lost
the car and me and probably herself as well
went all shaky and white, grey like the day
soon surrounded by policemen
materialized from the mists with notebooks
AA men with motor bikes, other drivers,
were asked a load of questions, quite fun.
Had to sit in unprepossessing room
unwelcome lull, inordinately dull
waiting for puncture to be mended
missed my dancing class.

Years later
relating this incident again en famille
when I got to the bit where
my mother threw her arms round me
she suddenly came to life and said with vigour,
“Oh no, Jenny, you’ve got that wrong
I could never have taken my hands
off the steering wheel at such a moment,”
Being grown-up and
prepared to capitulate to my dear mother
I said, “Oh I’m sorry, Ma,
I must be mistaken after so long.”
But I was sure I wasn’t.

Play us Something, Rosie

Oh no, I'd rather not
Of course you must, we're all longing to hear
You're not. You don't want to hear at all.
Yes we do, don't we? Appeals to friends.
We'd love to hear Rosie play, wouldn't we?
Hands spread, she looks from side to side.
Of course we would, lovely, oh yes, yes of course
Please Rosie, play something.

Rosie did not, in her own estimation, play well.
Notes were there, effect lumpy, unbeautiful
she did not like the sounds she made
but could not at present do any better
because she was only eleven and not a prodigy
it was, she knew, a hypocritical chorus
they did not want to hear her
except for suspect reasons, curiosity probably
or kindness, some sort of social custom
which she deplored, wouldn't listen, talk throughout
she was up in arms, indignant, reluctant.

What a fuss, Rosie, just play something
glare from mother who *would* not understand
Oh all right, sits down with a thump
What do you want me to play?
Oh anything darling
Your little Bach piece, perhaps
Little Bach piece, two-part invention
mini-masterpiece belonging to itself
related in all its angles
she may not play it well
but she does appreciate it.
Everyone looking at her. She begins.

Instantly they relax, turn back into their circle
begin to chat. Child is furious
cannot bear it, stops suddenly
rises to her feet. I won't play, she announces
and rushes from the room.
Brother, silent until now, follows her
up the stairs two at a time
who on earth do you think you are,
Rachmaninov?
Of course not, of course not.
Why do they want me to play and not listen?
It is rude to the music.

Ride to Pencrebar

Arrive on bicycle at top
of steep Newbridge Hill.
Some way down
on other side of road, entrance
to beautiful wooded Pencrebar drive
sloping up, a lane, gate never shut.

Freewheel down hill, no brakes
rather risky, rather silly, tut tut,
whip across road, through gate
see how far up you could get
without pedalling, stop when you had to
and wait for next.

Once I whizzed past car coming down
alarmed faces looking out
for years we played this competitive game
without our elders knowing anything about it
and now, of course, they never will
just as well, don't you think?

Bentleys

Of all the cars we had when I was young
I loved the Bentleys best, better than the rest
we had two, from the twenties
one three litre, the other four and a half
and many of their parts were interchangeable.
Father cannibalized them, several years
through the early thirties spent spare hours
swapping their insides about, his kind of fun
made him consistently late for meals
checking carburettors, concentrating on clutches
perusing plugs and pistons, fiddling with gears
rectifying restoring and renewing
thousand and one other small attentions
refreshing and reviving their energies.
At last, when one was as good as it could get
the other still working, still usable
still fit to be someone else's pet
he sold it for £12 to an enthusiast
who tinkered with it for a time in his turn
hurtled it round Brooklands, round and again
it had an outside brake and an old bulb horn
which reverberated with unmistakable point
Dad kept that.
Meanwhile, racing Bentleys at Brooklands
British racing green, of course, were a factor
ever-present in the distance, immensely glamorous
Speed Sixes, for instance, oh oh
holding on to their 'glorious tradition'
one driver, Tim Birkin, splendid Irishman
holds permanent record the old circuit
89.66 miles per hour in 1930.
It must be said, they had large engines
and won over and over, sometimes one two three
until Rudolf Caracciola came on the scene
driving a car designed by, guess who —
Doctor Porsche: after that what battles.

Well, they were beautiful cars.
Ours were red, that dark Bentley red
Bentley 'B' on the radiators
dignified knock-out dash, no bling
engine noise deep bass rumble, roar at speed
spoiled me for ever for the scream
of modern Grand Prix engines
though they are exciting too.
Impossible adequately to describe
Bentleys of those days, they just were
and in some cases still are.
Three Cheers.

Bentleys II

Father's efforts at cannibalizing
his two Bentleys, mostly a success
were not wholly without hazard.
Once, car outside door waiting to go
I leapt unconcernedly
from granite step across pavement
running jump into back
I was only eleven
burst through floor, splintering smash
landed on road, foot each side of silencer
brother, already aboard, observed coolly,
"Dad's not going to be pleased about that."
Clambered out in some distress, conscience-stricken
met him in hall, gasped, "Daddy - daddy -"
"Gently my love, gently." was all he said
presumably he'd heard the crash
had to wait while he mended it, started late
not unusual fate
last minute jiggling and juggling
spasmodic engine roars, lion in garage.

Another time
long journey up to Hampshire
he'd removed springs under back seat
no time to put them back, he said
not showing much insight
every time we went over a bump
back axle rose, shattering thump
I, well padded, not fat mind
survived relatively unbothered
but poor little brother, skinny little mite
honed by arduous prep school life
couldn't sit down for a week, it's true it's true
"I never really forgave him for that,"
he said morosely in later years,
"he could have done me lasting damage."
But he didn't.

Bentleys III

Sometimes on Sundays after breakfast
with pasties, large, hot from oven
well-wrapped, smelling of heaven
guaranteed to quell the lustiest appetite
we'd arrange ourselves and dogs of course
in whichever car was working best
and head for the Cornish coast
far as we could go and back in one day
hither and yon, stopping where we pleased
swimming, novelty or view
in those days, except August, visitors fairly few.
One of father's ideas, tide out
set steering wheel just so
leave car circling by itself on sand
once he got it wrong
car dug itself deep and deeper channel
had to be towed out by tractor
oh dear, poor dad, ignominious
we kept our mouths shut.
Another, terrifying this one
brinkmanship, don't think that word
had been invented then
first, get us all in as usual
more or less peacefully disposed
then, turning on cliff or quayside
drive slowly back .... and back
until wheels were almost at the edge
mother begging him to for heaven's sake
behave himself
trying not to think of drop beneath -
no doubt he had assured himself beforehand
of those imponderables, measurements, edges
but....

Often on way home racing in the dark
brother and I huddled on floor at back
with dogs, spaniels
clad in double everything, wrapped in rugs
sometimes over our heads, unable to see
hearing only the occasional whoosh
of something coming the other way
we were frozen, absolutely frozen with cold
Queen Victoria's pronouncement,
"Cold is good for you." Don't know
if she meant as cold as that
did she?
But we never complained, never thought of it
dare say they were none too warm in front
life was tough in open cars, tough fun
it did not seem to do us any harm
we lived to freeze another day.

April 1940
eye-witness account

We had been conscious for some time
of uneven bumps and bangs
guns of ships at sea, perhaps?
Naval battle far away?
Telephone rang for my father
Home Guard grapevine informed him
Germans bombing Plymouth.
He told us, expressionless voice
added after a pause
“This is history in the making
we’d better take a look.”
Drove to base of Kitt Hill
from where we could see Plymouth
fifteen or twenty miles away
across fields and the Tamar
mother, father, brother and me.
Appalling sight, blood-chilling.
Others gathered, speechless also
moonless night.
High above Plymouth, enormous pall of smoke
pitch black, solid, blacker than sky.
Below, black shafted red, red clouds,
from ground, flames, vivid bright scarlet flames
rising to great height, hideous huge bonfire
Plymouth burning, oh poor Plymouth
playground since birth
sharp knife in brain, lasting ugly bruise.
Unseen planes, distant engine noise, like our own
they flew straight across, I suppose
and went back to Germany
but to distraught teenage senses
it seemed they circled the helpless city
already a holocaust
dead bodies, smashed bodies, buried bodies
imagined screams and shouts.

Sky full of objects, falling at different speeds
downward path lit by flames
Molotov Cocktails in holders, bucketing
cheerily down with savage intent, landmines
deliberately drifting, attached to parachutes
landing with frightful force
earth tremble miles away, under our feet
bombs, incendiaries, burning bits and pieces
vision of hell, let loose indeed
what barbarity
that one country could treat another so
what barbarity
I thought then that all Germans were monsters
mindless monsters.

WRNS Quarters, Wartime

Number 4, Penlee Gardens
Stoke, Devonport, Plymouth, still there
commandeered then, one presumes
from its owners for the duration
as most houses in the row
solid, large, Victorian
in front wide path, grassed-over slope
gardens at back.
I seem to remember Number 8
was where we ate (beef all right
roast potatoes solid with fat
soaked in it, pale pale ugh
one egg a week, Sunday morning,
dried egg least said)
must have had many breakfasts there
but don't remember a single one
perhaps dashed in and out, seizing piece of bread
never much good in the mornings.
Number 11, I believe, was Admin,
pay forty two shillings a fortnight
to begin with.
Notices, fire watching rotas
travel warrants, that sort of thing
trouble if you got in late
ten thirty deadline, eleven o'clock
once a month, late night pass.
Ruled over by Quarters Chief Petty Officer
small neat lady
something of a grandee in my book
competent, fair, agreeable, stern
commanding respect in heads
perhaps a trifle overbold
young and spirited
it's my guess she settled for being Chief
all through the war, turned down
a commission, a jewel indeed.

We had a girl once in our cabin
didn't wash, never had a bath, pretty girl
after some weeks we began to worry
they gave her a bath by force
one Saturday morning
washed her clothes too, some of them
apparently she yelled a lot
did her no good, everybody out
except the purposeful few
quarters staff took a hand: she went.
Once we had a prostitute
someone saw her in civilian clothes
unmistakable, they said
she did us no harm
but she didn't last long either
once we had an intruder
but that's another story
We did not spend much time there
generally humdrum
our real lives outside.

Admiral

At far end of terrace
in which we lived, Penlee Gardens
house of an Admiral
a balcony
and perhaps in the summer
geraniums.

We were asked to respect his presence
and so we did.
stopped our occasional perambulations
up and down the row
short of his dwelling
did not walk in front.

We never saw him, not a glimpse
didn't know his name
he was reputed to be retired
old and ill dying perhaps
one must respect an Admiral
his presence lends grandeur
and glamour.

Wartime Footwear

"Do you want some shoes?"
asked my mother, a note of doubt
in her voice.
I was on leave at the time.
"What are they like?" I asked warily.
"Well," she said, "they were made
by a friend of Mr Ferris
and he kindly offered me some."
Mr Ferris was the manager of our local co-op
lived with his family top floor of our house
his having been blitzed, wartime arrangement.
"They're rather colourful," she added.
Colourful they certainly were
remnants of suede
large patches blue scarlet turquoise
no two colours touching
flat-heeled lace-ups, blunt toes
red shoe laces, wooden soles.
My mother had bought two pairs
one pair scarlet, turquoise and blue
the other turquoise blue and scarlet
we gazed at them silently.
"Well, thank you," I said, "I, er -
I can't quite make up my mind."
"No, I can't either," she agreed,
"they're only five pounds."
"Well perhaps they're rather fun
are they?"
"Either fun or impossible."
"Well, I'll have a pair and find out."

Having One's Hair Done

Plymouth after the blitz
hairdressers in short supply
found one, advertisement in paper
private house, outskirts
my friend Dorothy and I
in our civvies, bent on luxury
headed that way one Saturday morning
I wearing astonishing shoes, wooden soles
obtained by mother from unknown source
frightfully slippery
could only go uphill
with precarious skating motion.

Ordinary little house, we found
semi-detached
path up through garden
as we approached gate
began to pour with rain
cloudburst no less, cats and dogs
Dorothy led, I trying to hurry
in my weird shoes
feet shot from under me
hit her briskly behind knees
landed sitting upright, very tidy
she on all fours
shape we made reminded me
of a modern sculpture.

Path, flagged, concreted
stone-edged, waterproofed
rain made it a rushing river
downhill, several inches deep
I laughed and laughed
Dorothy irritated, understandably so
It poured and poured
Shoes so slippery, oh dear.

"Do get up Jenny," she said trying to help
I laughing too much, slipping
sliding about, ankle deep
oh dear, seldom laughed more.

We staggered into house,
Dripped, streamed copiously in hall
"Tut tut," they said astonished
took our skirts off
and our shoes and stockings and jackets
well everything, really
wrapped us in towels
front room turned into
sort of hairdressing salon
wartime emergency measure
still looked like living room
obviously was in the evenings
armchairs, ornaments, false flowers,
hairdryers hid behind curtains
washbasins anchored to walls
behind screens
we sat there wrapped in towels
as if we had been swimming.

Having One's Hair Done II

We had different programmes
Dorothy, wash and set
I a 'perm' which took longer, much longer
never had one before
Dee brought her library book
to occupy her while she waited
it was very exciting, blonde heroine
all the accoutrements, big blue eyes
well-behaved, well brought up
her beloved 'ran' silk, tea, spirits
for the benefit of the population
Cornish I suspect
gently born, of course, wildly handsome
black hair, the lot, a Lord at least
every now and then I asked
how they were doing
sometimes one or both got wet
it's a built-in risk when doing
that sort of thing
and seemed to us, in our towels
frightfully funny, oh dear
quite worn out with laughing
hairdressing staff, all two of them
were infected
my hair turned out simply awful
so thickly curled
could not get a comb through it
for about a week
had to wear a hat all the time
never had another
oh dear, the whole thing
was hilarious

Wartime Clothing

You could buy furnishing fabric
coupon free all through the war
more or less
a dicey undertaking, seemed to me
mattress ticking, jacket perhaps
rather chic: skirt as well
made you a bit of a freak
if you were the slightest bit fat
(I wasn't) looked like a pillow
or a mattress even
that's enough of that.

Cretonne a definite risk, and chintz
one did not wish
to resemble a sofa, plum and quince
or loose-covered armchair
large flowers and birds
nor want one's skirt to flutter
in such a way
as to cause passers-by to mutter
Good heavens
she's wearing the curtains.

But black-out material
full skirt made for dancing
six yards, mid-calf
double hem for swing
top, embroidered white dress
offered by sympathetic aunt
twenties, I suppose, treasured ever since
wide hem, flower embroidered,
transferred to frill round neck
fell to elbows
pale blue sash, or scarlet
not half bad.

Wartime Clothing II

Later on
parachutes became available
silk for a wedding dress
or underwear
bought one, desperate unpicking
finally cut inside seams
and armed with a number of tapering pieces
floaty nightdresses, I hoped
arrived at house of friend
whose mother, she said,
had a sewing machine.
Unfortunately it turned out
to be old-fashioned, treadle type
an antique.
took several visits to master it
using old bits of sheet -
Then, after all that
it wouldn't sew parachute silk
kept tripping over itself
rucked it up, so to speak
gave up whole idea
and handed pieces to friend.

Wartime Car

For AHB with love

My father's car
which he drove throughout the war
was a BMW, German
one of the first half dozen
to come into the country
nineteen thirty six, CRL2,
Viscount Clifden beat him to CRL1.

Middle of war, dark night
Home Guard put ancient bayonet
through fabric of roof
"Oh I'm sorry, sir
didn't mean to do that,"
he said much abashed
it was grievously slashed.

For the rest of the war
who sat in back
sheltered under an umbrella
when it rained
nothing to mend it with
my father said
nothing else for it.

Unwelcome Presence

Eight of us in our cabin
No 4 Penlee Gardens
ground floor at back
personnel constantly shifted
atmosphere remained convivial
I, living nearby in Cornwall
often went home at weekends
sometimes taking with me
one of the eight, bus train bus
twenty-five miles across border.

One week when I returned
they began telling me
there had been — an intruder!
It was awfully scary, Jenny
in the middle of the night
I bet it was, what did you do?
They couldn't do much
because of the black-out, you see
couldn't switch on the light, of course
apparently he went away.

Next week he came again,
same day, Saturday
again I was missing
couldn't think how he got in
cabin with French window
no other ventilation
opening to back garden deserted
once lovely, no doubt
now neglected space, weeds
high walls all round, eight or ten feet
he must be agile.

Well you are a spiritless lot
I told them cheerfully
next week I'll stay here, I said
we'll give him a shock, I said
now let me see, we must rush him
I'll cast myself to the floor
grab him round the knees
with a witchy shriek
bring him down, like Rugby
that'll teach him a lesson.

You, I said, picking the smallest
blonde skating ballerina from Blackpool
shine a torch
so that we know where we are
You, I continued, choosing a girl
of Welsh farming stock, solid
must sit on him, sit on his chest
I won't be here, said another anxiously
it's my long weekend, I'll be away
Oh what a pity, never mind,

yes, well, where were we - that leaves four
you two, I said, friends
office-workers from Birmingham
sit on his legs, one leg each
the other two sit on his arms
all of you scream as loud as you can
Got that? Oh, I added
one of you threaten him with the poker,
fireplace in cabin
still fire - irons, quite handsome

We had one or two rehearsals
before lights out, hilarious
Joyce ex-hairdresser from Leeds
especially impressive with the poker
instructions not to hit
might hit one of us
we couldn't practise screaming
hoped it would come naturally.
Finally came Saturday.
We weren't a bit frightened.

Joyce went to bed with the poker
suitably cleansed
we left French window open as usual
tried to stay awake, very difficult
I fancy we all went to sleep
all of a sudden a deep voice out of the black
a-a-a-ah, Wrens!
educated voice, incredibly sinister
you could just see him silhouetted
darker shape against dark night.

As one we all sat bolt upright
me included,
and screamed our heads off
no difficulty about that.
Quarters came to life
all sorts of people came from all over
in their nighties and pyjamas, hair in curlers
demanding to know whatever —
He had gone of course
and never came again.

Near Miss

There we were in a passage
bare boards, ground floor
Penlee Gardens, No 4
air raid middle of night
crash pause crash pause
apparently designed for every other house.
Always tried to stay in bed
warm and comfortable at least
with a pillow for my head
routed out by Petty Officer
wretched woman, doing her duty
so sat in passage with others
leaning against wall
dull and cold, longing for sleep
suddenly a different noise
rush past, ground-shaking thud
what was that?
Momentary interest
followed by weary wait.
Next morning we found German bomber
crashed, surprisingly small
no signs of pilot, no blood
would have wished him dead, no doubt
missed teeming WRNS Quarters
by a few feet, literally
landed on grassy slope in front
they put a guard on wreck, rather late
citizens of Plymouth, somehow alerted
carried off bits and pieces
as souvenirs
where it landed, it dug itself a great hole
a grave.

Years Later

Visiting cousins in Penlee Gardens
one said, “Jenny I believe in the war
a German bomber crashed here?”
“Oh yes,” I said, “I was present at the time.”
“Could you remember, do you think
exactly where it landed?”
“I’m sure I could, let’s look.”
Good heavens. A short way along
in the smooth contours of the bank
there was the hole.
An uneven pit, grassed over now
glossed over, so to speak
not as deep
but unmistakeable.

Little Person

I only encountered a little person once
ages ago.
By that I mean
a perfectly formed person of restricted growth.
I was with a favourite aunt
who noticed that he was smoking
Oh dear, look at that little boy, Jenny
he is smoking a cigarette
oh dear, I must say something to him.
You really should not be smoking
at your age, you know
It is terribly bad for you.
He looked at her
ordinary trousers and sweater
Do you suppose it will stunt my growth?
He enquired with perfect courtesy
in a man's voice
I am grown up, Madam, I am twenty-four.
He walked away.
She was absolutely disconcerted
she had meant well.

New Plymouth

Around the end of WW II
in Alexandria, I saw the plans
and their architect who had come
to interpret them to anyone interested.
To my unskilled eye
they seemed O.K, quite exciting
I was quite enthused
as was architect
but when I saw the reality
later in the rain
it was dark grey concrete
and cream-coloured roses, dripping.

Next Car

Very pretty, this one

When he had driven his BMW
for ten or so years
he changed it after the war
for a real good-looker
handsome Talbot 110
110 brake horsepower, that is
spectacularly graceful and quiet
gadget on steering wheel
pre-selector gears.
Belonged at first to old lady
who used her almost never
then demonstration car, London showroom
and Olympia Motor Show
she'd still only done twenty miles
when Pa caught up with her
a slow starter.
He taught me to drive
in and out of the lanes
whisking along the straights
crawling round the corners
with caution, horn sounding
not much use with double de-clutching
still going strong in cars of friends.
Started little brother, now full size
on his lifelong hobby, Talbots
which he collected from all over
in all sorts of conditions
he had twelve at one point
or even thirteen
restoring and racing them,
winning prizes, selling them again
writing about them
you name it.

Pa’s personable princess
(oh dear, sentimentality
must stamp on myself)
is still around, still going strong
restored several times by now, I should think
for sale at 95½ thousand.

Hard Going

In Ireland we lived
in an old house on an island
across a causeway
thousands of swans when startled
or when they thought they would
took to the air
wheeled and freewheeled
in arcs and swirls, most beautiful
house miles from anywhere
empty for twenty years
no electricity, no phone
almost an hour every evening
to light lamps.
I called it 'Wormwood Scrubs'.
A well in back yard, no spring
no water till it rained
tank from a roof
not enough, not enough.
We had a baby.
Stream which dried up in summer
some way down lane
a spring, little pond
from which the cows drank
you could fill buckets
if you had to.
My husband
thought it was lovely
but if you sat on a beach
they threw stones at you
he, part Irish, had a simple answer
don't sit on it
it was possible to think.
Don't live here.

Ghost

She woke up suddenly
and knew she was not alone in the room
husband away, Duty Officer
nursemaid and baby across landing
black of night
curtains open to outside
no light came in
only Ireland which she loved
to this uneasy house
became conscious of slight glimmer
on bedside table
oh, how silly, she thought
bedside lamp not turned off properly
oil lamp, small
even as she thought it
glimmer developed, clarified
into little old lady
sitting up beside her in double bed
wore a frilly nightcap
shawl round her shoulders, pince nez
looked down at her
severe expression as if to say
"And what are you doing in my bed
young woman?"
Jenny was taken aback
no time for fright
quick, quick as a flash
she began the Lord's Prayer
when she had got through it once
the apparition was still there
began a second time
slowly it swung round forty-five degrees
as slowly faded
Jenny felt flustered, to say the least
but on the whole she thought
best thing to do

go to sleep again
which she did quite soon
she guessed who it was
old lady who had owned the house
two or three generations ago
and was reputed to love it
“How she could —” thought Jenny
who didn’t.
Next evening, husband back
no spectre would trifle with him, she thought
but she was never discomfited
by anything spooky again
she had found the answer, you see.

Irish Weather

The butcher arrived
parked in back yard
splashed through puddles
gloom and drizzle
past enormous turf pile
up thirteen steps
to kitchen door
and remarked,
“It’s a lovely day, ma’am
but the rain is terrible.”

Invited Hardships

Why do people choose
to make themselves suffer
put themselves through it?
They're curious, I suppose
to show they can do it
prove to themselves
that they're quite a bit tougher
can take everything
much harder and rougher
than the ordinary home-loving
woman or man
demonstrate that
if they want to they can.
They toil across deserts
with slightly cross camels
and struggle through jungles
with spiders and snakes
they cross over torrents
on tremulous bridges
a proud overcoming
not only of rivers
but most understandable
shakings and shivers
oh most comprehensible
quakings and quivers.
They scramble up mountains
with insecure toe-holds
to unskilled eyes
there appear to be no-holds
find themselves threatened
by blood-sucking leeches
by poisonous insects
and dangerous beaches
they trouble themselves

with tortuous teases
and make themselves ill
with foreign diseases
get lost and exhausted
and go without sleep
for no tangible reason
just a memory to keep
and all the time saying
how much they enjoy it
if they have common sense
they don't seem to employ it.
Now let me suggest
that the painters and makers
the builders, constructors
designers, creators
are no less challenged
than all these others
their desperately daring
sisters and brothers
a blank page or canvas
a workshop location
can be a severely demanding test
a matter of thinking
no dodging or shrinking
just how the hell
you can do your best.

Antonio Vivaldi
1676 - 1741

So brilliantly evokes his city
at all seasons as the world knows
sometimes at night, late
trills on flute, magic instrument
or shakes would you rather
long as the breath holds
last few moments a little edgy
walk among water
tall buildings both sides
deserted pavements
fragmenting moon, cloud-crossed
door opens
party, splendid array
dancing, torrent of chat
resplendent unnatural blondes
rooftops all day
Venetian stuff,
ciscisbeos, masks, glass
outside again silence
no one about
sleeping state, shadowed, spooky
Venice has always leaned a bit
in that direction.

Name

Embroidery course
went to many
hard work, great fun
sat round table, about ten
mostly strangers to each other
stated our names one by one
so we all knew who we were
when it was my turn
I announced myself
silence fell.
“Well, it’s not unusual, is it?”
I said, wondering,
the opposite was true
everybody knew
a Jenefer Murray
all different
that’s why I call myself
Jenefer Ann Murray
Because if at all possible
One must be distinct.

Little Beau

My car
I had a car
one car which I loved
beyond all the rest
silver, sleek, sparky, spirited
incomparably dear and dashing
infinitely welcoming and willing
cocoon against the world
Scirocco Mark 1, fuel injection
androgynous as her name suggests
if written - Little Beau Peep-Peep
for me top billing
oh yes, I loved her best
drove her before and after life turned black
getaway from tears, which came too
there's no escape, bur slightly mitigated
reminded myself that there were
other things in life besides sorrow
most of us know something of that
tomorrow and tomorrow and tomorrow
I drove her for seventeen years
up and down the country
fleeted and flighted along the motorways
no sense of direction you see
passing whom we pleased without effort
letting the mercedes and jaguars go gracefully by
sounds of her engine - sublime
magnificent roars on demand
like a little lion but smoother, technical
or Pavarotti I idiotically thought
oh, I loved her and paid the price
for loving what is not made to last
things, animals, people
sometimes one's dear children
yet 'tis better to have loved -
is it not?

Holiday Weekend

Once upon a time
I came down from London
in the faithful and untiring
Little Beau, my car
Friday evening Bank Holiday
not an enormous amount of traffic
no blocks, spaces between
became aware
something in the air
everybody flying to get there
holiday, hooray
slow lane going at eighty
middle lane at ninety
fast lane at goodness knows what
charging along
some with finger on horn - continuous blare
tried it myself for a mile or two
exciting, whoopee
so we all flew along, unhindered,
in 1983.

Foggy Foggy Night

Once upon a time
I left London in the faithful
and tireless Little Beau, my car
straight from work, misty evening
paused for food at motorway caff
about second one down
plenty of people
leisurely, no hurry, relax
emerged into fog, thick, thick, the thickest
could hardly retreat to London
might miss a turning, be lost
carried on down motorway
at first, some company
soon drifted away, nobody going far
all alone, still can feel the thrill
drove along, middle lane, slow
just see markings on one side or other
once I stopped, switched off engine
take a rest, savour the world
Cathedral silence, everything blanketed, rolled up
enjoying as I did
Little Beau, motorways and myself
an idyllic, magic experience
totally unfrequented road, just the three of us
switch on again, two hundred mile journey
more or less secure between boundaries
slowly creeping, faster than snail
sometimes singing, tra la.
At length, brainswept, peaceful
I arrived, small sense of achievement
husband and son burst from house
noisy and cross
"Where have you been?
What have you been *DOING?*"
"Have you gone mad?"

Oh God, nearly turned round
and went back
not very late, about eleven I suppose.

Apparently radio said, no travelling
Keep off roads.
Never listen to car radio
don't know how anybody can.
Riunously distorted music.

Merely a Wreck

I looked after that car, kept her trim,
when I came here
she was already ten years old
had to park in the road
before making a space
in the garden among the flowers
a sentimental way of putting it
I know, I know
her sidelights were smashed
more than once
people banged into them when backing
side mirror swept askew
badge burgled, brand image
perennially stolen from Sciroccos
by naughty young
saw them from bedroom window
girl turned up laughing face, pretty girl,
could not get downstairs in time
tell them I was a Cornish witch
declamatory, dramatic, wild,
"I put a curse on you
may you never be happy
until you are sorry for this."
Got another badge which I cherish still
her roof was trampled in, middle of one night
not broken, merely deformed
could be mended, hammered out again.
Eventually she had to go, too old
too expensive to run, unreliable at last
sold her, thirty pieces of silver it felt like
young man from a garage, he was delighted
his favourite model
I sobbing, sobbing, ridiculous
so miserable, oh hell
"Mrs Murray," he said impatiently
"do go and get yourself a cup of tea."

Cried for her all that afternoon
only once, it seemed permissible
I did not have to seem brave
like I was before
like when the children went, or my brother
was not, as then, broken-hearted
merely a wreck

Designed by Giorgetto Gingaro

If it's not Right, it's Wrong

First the idea
Write it down
blank side business letter
back of old calendar
preserved for this purpose
bend to your will
round and round racetrack
up and down hill
polish and hone
interruption, 'phone
hello darling, how are you?
yes I'm busy too
rapid return
word's wrong doesn't belong
awkward sound, cracked gong
delete, lop, don't hesitate
extra words dilute
unflavour the fruit
hone and polish
develop and demolish
addition, subtraction
Capital letter distraction
oh hell, front door bell
parcel to sign for
back to desk
sadly humdrum word
replace at once
with another less often heard
change tense
improvement immense
or not - don't know what -
oh yes, that's right
getting dark switch on light
rhythm lumpy and bumpy
unintentional, insupportable
twist about, smooth out

chequered flag in sight
in the end, if right
gleam for you, silver and gold
thousandth time read over
brain in clover
begin another
more fish in the river

The Car My Father Had After That

Donald Campbell's dark blue Bristol
The one he drove to Coniston Water
and left behind
I think he knew
Coniston Water would overthrow him
that it was not reliable that day
could not wait longer
or back out
bound by circumstance
poor Donald Campbell
beautiful car.

Somewhere Else

One day when I was driving somewhere
on my way to somewhere else
I saw approaching
an elegant old man
driving a gorgeous car
Donald Campbell's dark blue Bristol
it was my father
we just had time to wave
and then we were both going
somewhere else.

Grief Poem V

My son, precious older son
conceived in bliss and joy
precautions taken in vain
carried in extreme sickness
frustration and upset
disliked and resented by his father
throughout childhood
by his mother beloved
handsome, stormy, determined,
a force with many talents
by himself hardly appreciated
now for many years estranged
I suppose I should have expected it
but I didn't
step by step unseeing.

Ships That Pass

The telephone rang
it was ten o'clock at night
"OO'S THIS THEN?"
enquired a large warm voice
with all the significance
all the meaning in the world.
"I'm afraid I can't guess."
I replied with a giggle.
Pause
"Oh, arn't you my sister-in-law then?"
Evident disappointment.
"Afraid not."
"I must've got the wrong number."
"Afraid so. Hard luck."
"What part of the world are you from, then, dear?"
"I live in Newquay now."
Pause.
"That's where I started from."
"Did you. Well, I'm sorry I'm not your sister-in-law."
"So'm I, dear."
"Bye bye."
Click.

Plain Girl

Saw a girl today
ornaments in her hair
streamed down her back
coloured bits and pieces
all different
not a pretty girl
heavy features
rather fat, no make-up
shabby clothes
but the hair, lovely
shone in the sun
glittered gently
don't know
how it was done

It’s a Wrap
for Stephen Curtis

This Christmas
as well as all the rest
I saw a ravishing motor car
most drop-dead gorgeous car
I’ve ever seen
dark British racing green
almost black
great big spare wheel along one side
Frazer Nash 1950 Le Mans racer
could not tell you how it works
about its quips and quirks
if it’s got any
and I dare say it has
can be driven on the road
went to Italian Alps last summer
British man-made ace
twisted my heart
gave brain a jolt
made me think
I could go out in the rain
and sing
yes, like the song says
go out singing and dancing
in the rain.

Another Five Fragments

XI

A particular blue
seen somewhere last September
you thought it indescribable then
and now you can't remember

XII

If Shakespeare could do it
and what a lot he did
I can break a few conventions
and not do what I'm bid

XIII

I think the world of you, you know
said his voice on the telephone
her soul stepped lightly up
another rung of the ladder

XIV

When she was a small child
she seemed like a toy
which brought joy
wherever it went

XV

A fine thing to do, friend
when you are getting old
is to buy a good wristwatch
to stand as a barrier
between yourself
and confusion.
not the kind that takes
a load of money and
three months to service.

Can This be England?

Latest deprivation
cricket on television
except on some obscene channel
which I am unable to find
Otherwise, it seems, I pay
never done that before.
Unable now to follow
course of a single wicket
and I do very much mind
dammit I was brought up on it.
Attended cricket matches
from early age while mother knitted
summertime in the unmown outback
where balls never came
keeping an eye on the action
unique,
silent finger, irrefutable
flying bails, run out, LBW, carrying bat
loved watching it
listening to it, crack of ball, how's that
didn't like playing it though
school, dull.
Father explained the game to me
in all its million nuances
no good now, I can't watch
shame, those peaceful days
cooking, ironing, painting the banisters
or whatever, telly switched on
to cricket freeing the mind
in its inimitable way

Other Birds

Vex not thy spirit at the course of things
they heed not thy vexation.
Marcus Aurelius

As well as the seagulls
here by the sea
crows, who stand about
by rubbish bags on Tuesdays
looking as if they owned them
strutting proud
spasmodically picking, like gulls
letting loose horrid flood
last week, twenty-seven paper plates
round white afflictions, imagine
in my front garden, blown in.
Window cleaner helped me pick them up
or I helped him
there, that didn't take long, he said
as we straightened up again
kind of him, soothed my spirits
which had become irrationally vexed
in spite of advice, age old.
There are blackbirds, two
which sit on our television aerials
and will so beautifully sing
in the spring
jackdaws in our disused chimney pots
savage creatures
alas they lie in wait
to grab small starlings when they venture out
and eat them, such is Mother Nature
starlings in the autumn
tightly wheeling phalanxes
ordered dots in the distance
an occasional robin one intrepid wagtail
sparrows, a failing breed it seems
still here and little wrens
down by the harbour on the cliffs.

Goddaughter's Sister

She came to see me yesterday
wearing pink and white trainers, lace-ups,
turquoise stockings, smooth, smooth
divided skirt, drab, calf-length
large red and white sweater
large red stripes across
and her fair hair fell straight

That is what I call well-dressed.

Orphan

Poor Indian child
lives rough, runs wild
on the pavements
of the overflowing city
dangerous, glamorous
menaced by adults
desperate or evil
and other kids alike
free amongst deprivation
degradation, starvation
disordered in the dust
at risk
use your wits, look out
or else.

Poor British child
ranked and filed
in an orphanage
disciplined, drab and dull
singularly undiverted
threatened by adults
and other kids alike
haughty or naughty
angry or perverted
imprisoned by necessity
outlook void and null
supposedly safe
use your wits, obey the rules
or else.

Elegy

I shall come to your funeral
and I shall cry silently
all the way through, I expect
tears will slide down my face
escaping the too-small handkerchief
held to my eyes
crunched up in my hand
with my spectacles
I will sing now and then
when I can
in a wavering voice, gulping
I shall be sad
but also glad
that I have known you
for a long time
and have you in my mind
lifesize
I salute you, lovely friend
for being as you were.

Some Time After

Now that she has allowed herself at last
to feel resentment about her husband
more and more arrives as if by every post
piles in like a tsunami
she standing now outside, above
as if on balcony
regarding the raging waters in turmoil below
full of trouble, full of rubble
knocked about in memory still

Phone Call

Alexander rang from America
my grandson, I love it when he rings
hell's teeth, bad line, cut off
tried again, cut off again
oh my poor heart
He managed to tell me
that his new thing is furniture making
so delighted, runs in the family
both sides
he is rebelling, he says,
against furniture too small
he is six feet four or five
and has made a tall black bed
I am sure it is handsome
probably witty as well
what is he making now?
I want to hear more
what next, what next?
Alex of the black bed
hell's teeth I shall have to wait.

Other books by Jenefer Ann Murray:

The First Fifty Poems	ISBN 978-0-9556682-3-4
The Second Fifty Poems	ISBN 978-0-9556682-7-2
The Third Fifty Poems	ISBN 978-1-906845-05-6
The Fourth Fifty Poems	ISBN 978-1-906845-07-0